THE NEWSIES

A Brief History of How Orphaned Boys Defeated Two Powerful Newspaper Moguls

HISTORY ENCOUNTERS

HISTORY ENCOUNTERS

The Newsies

A Brief History of How Orphaned Boys Defeated Two Powerful Newspaper Moguls

Contents

Preview Introduction

A massive strike stopped the circulation of newspapers in New York City just before the turn of the twentieth century. However, neither the strikers nor the majority of the parties involved were professionals. Young boys, known as "newsboys," led the charge in "The Newsboys' Strike of 1899," pitting themselves against newspaper magnates like William Randolph Hearst and Joseph Pulitzer.

Chapter One: Introduction

On the streets of New York City in 1899, you could hear the Newsboys' voices over the din. Once upon a time, the city's main news source was the printed newspaper. There was no other way to learn about global events. The New York World and the New York Journal were the two main newspapers that changed hands. Joseph Pulitzer and William Randolph Hearst, two of New York's most influential men, owned them. In common parlance, newspapers cost "a dime a paper."

The Newsboys were largely homeless youth and abandoned children. They had nowhere to go and nobody to see, so they slept on the streets of New York. They relied only on newspaper sales to make ends meet as they moved from one New York street corner to another. The money they made selling newspapers was all they had to buy food, shelter, and other necessities, and they had to save part of it so they could buy more newspapers to sell the next day. To increase their paper sales, these Newsboys needed to be exceptionally convincing. So, if a Newsboy didn't make their quota the previous day, they wouldn't be able to make it up the next day. In other words, they were deprived of food and other necessities for life.

New Yorkers were in for a pleasant surprise on an ordinary day. Everything changed on that particular day. Pulitzer and Hearst discussed their mutual desire to increase their wealth and came to the conclusion that they should work together. They proposed several solutions, such as reducing factory workers' pay (which would entail layoffs) and eliminating low-level positions altogether. Then someone had the bright notion of increasing the tax Newsboys pay on newspapers. It's official: the price of newspapers has increased from fifty to sixty cents. Even at this inflated price, the Newsboys barely broke even. The Newsboys were understandably distraught by this development. When the Newsies took a stand, it was the beginning of one of the most remarkable strikes (led by children).

In July 1899, many Newsboys boycotted Joseph Pulitzer's and William Randolph Hearst's publications. Over the course of many days, the strike spread to the Brooklyn Bridge, causing a major backup of traffic. It also stopped the distribution of Pulitzer and Hearst newspapers across New England. More than five thousand Newsboys from all across the city showed up for several rallies. Kid Blink, the strike's organizer, spoke at each and every event. Kid Blink, the young man who wore an eye patch because he was blind in one eye, was a familiar figure in New York City tabloids. Blink received widespread acclaim in the New York Tribune, which often cited him despite his distinctive Brooklyn accent. On occasion, Kid Blink and the Newsboys resorted to violence. Sometimes Pulitzer and Hearst had to break up protests and ensure the paper delivery was safe. Blink famously remarked to the strikers, "Colleagues and chums, all in one. This is a testing moment for men's emotional fortitude. At this point, we've got to be as close as glue… No matter how blind we are, we will still get what we desire."

Pulitzer and Hearst did not reduce their newspaper prices but pledged to buy back any unsold copies. This ultimately led to the dissolution of the Newsboys' union. A number of additional strikes occurred simultaneously or shortly afterward around the nation due to this first action. The Newsboys Strike of 1914 in Butte, Montana, and the Newsboys Strike of the 1920s in Louisville, Kentucky, are two such instances. Also, a few decades later, a new urban child-welfare technique was implemented, which ultimately enhanced the standard of living for the Newsboys.

The following parts explain why the strike occurred, what transpired during it, and the long-term consequences of this event. In sum, the strike demonstrates that everyone, regardless of age, appearance, social status, or background, can significantly impact the world if they set their minds to it and work toward that goal.

Chapter Two: Joseph Pulitzer

A portrait of Joseph Pulitzer.

Joseph Pulitzer was a newspaper magnate and reporter. Pulitzer oversaw the successful publishing of the New York World and the St. Louis Post-Dispatch. Hoping to recruit enthusiastic, dedicated journalists to the industry, Pulitzer left money in his will to create a school of journalism at Columbia University and the Pulitzer Prize.

Joseph Pulitzer was born in Mako, Hungary, on April 10, 1847.

Pulitzer's father was a rich grain merchant who reared him and his siblings in Budapest. Pulitzer was educated at an exclusive private school and had extra help from a tutor. After his father's death when he was seventeen, Pulitzer decided he wanted to join the military and applied to the Austrian Army. Despite being rejected because of his bad vision, he was eventually enlisted in Germany to fight for the Union. In 1864, he left Europe and settled in America. His postwar life began in St. Louis, Missouri, where he did a variety of professions until settling into his current profession as a reporter.

Pulitzer was so determined to join the army that he went to Germany to talk to a bounty hunter, who eventually conscripted him to fight for the Union in the Civil War. Legend has it that Pulitzer swam from a ship to the coast of Boston upon his arrival in the United States. He served with the Lincoln Cavalry for a year. He eventually settled in St. Louis, where he worked as a luggage handler and then a server. Next, he went to St. Louis's Mercantile Library to study English and the law. He started as a reporter at the Weistliche Post, a German daily, in 1868. While just 25 years old in 1872, Pulitzer had already established himself as a dedicated journalist with a stellar reputation. He invested in a stake in a German newspaper and eventually took over as publisher. Indeed, Pulitzer was a savvy businessman who, in 1878, combined the St. Louis Globe and the St. Louis Dispatch, two newspapers he had purchased. Pulitzer's career in journalism was only getting started when the St. Louis Post-Dispatch was established.

The Post-Dispatch spurred Pulitzer's desire to expand his journalistic reach. Pulitzer and his new bride moved to New

York in 1883, and he bought the struggling New York World from gangster Jay Gould. The World was quickly transformed into a phenomenon because of Pulitzer. He toiled at producing a journal that championed the ordinary man and labor rights. He accomplished this by advocating for workers' rights and using an investigative reporting technique to expose the rich's corruption in politics and fraud. With the inclusion of comedy, sports, and fashion coverage, Pulitzer aided in transforming newspapers into a form of entertainment and news source. That led to a rise in the newspaper's readership. Pulitzer worked tirelessly to ensure his newspaper reflected the interests of its readers.

Pulitzer's publications included serious exposés of governmental corruption, crusading investigative reporting, and more sensationalist pieces aimed at drawing attention to Pulitzer himself. Adding cartoons, sports coverage, women's fashion coverage, and graphics to his publications helped him attract a wider audience by making them more than just a source of news.

Nellie Bly was engaged as a reporter by Pulitzer in 1887. With her own investigation reporting, Bly aided Pulitzer in his support of the people. She assisted him with promotion efforts as well. In 1889, Bly approached Pulitzer about contributing to the cost of her circumnavigation. Pulitzer agreed, and the journey was made into a PR ploy by having participants estimate how long it would take Bly to go around the world. The New York World became the most widely read daily in the United States because of its combination of sensationalist and investigative reporting.

During his time in Missouri, Pulitzer stepped into the political arena. In 1869, he won a seat in the Missouri state legislature. He was instrumental in establishing the Liberal Republican Party, which backed Horace Greeley against Ulysses S. Grant for the presidency. However, over time, he shifted his political affiliation to the Democrats. The average person benefited from Pulitzer's investigative reporting and exposing political wrongdoing. Pulitzer used the World to assist in collecting money to replace the Statue of Liberty's stalled pedestal in France. It was Pulitzer's life's work to improve the quality of journalism.

Early in his career, Pulitzer fought against splashy headlines and artwork. Down the 1890s, when his competition with Hearst heated up, Pulitzer and Hearst both began using bigger headline types, more bizarre art, and dubious business tactics until Pulitzer finally chose to rein it in. However, Pulitzer stood by his tactics, arguing that education about crime was essential to reducing its prevalence. As he told one of his detractors, "I want to communicate to a country, not a select committee."

Chapter Three: William Randolph Hearst

William Randolph Hearst

A portrait of William Randolph Hearst.

His father's newspaper, the San Francisco Examiner, was floundering when William Randolph Hearst took over as publisher in 1887. By the 1930s, he had developed the nation's greatest media empire, comprising more than two dozen newspapers in major cities countrywide, periodicals, wire and picture services, newsreels, radio stations, and film production. Hearst, the first media mogul in the United States, was responsible for popularizing the sensationalist practices that would define modern news coverage.

A native of San Franciso, Hearst was born on April 29, 1863, to George Hearst, a Missouri mining mogul who had moved west during the Gold Rush, and Phoebe Apperson Hearst, a former schoolteacher who was also from Missouri. He attended Harvard University and was the business editor for the Harvard Lampoon before being kicked out of school for missing too many courses and other misdeeds.

While his father encouraged him to enter the mining sector, Hearst was determined to establish his reputation in the newspaper industry. The older Hearst, who was elected as a U.S. senator in 1886, had bought the San Francisco Examiner as a platform for his political career; inspired by the example of Joseph Pulitzer's New York World, William urged George to grant him the management of the paper.

At the young age of 24, Hearst used his family's wealth to hire the best newspaper talent of the day (including writers like Mark Twain, Ambrose Bierce, and Jack London), and he adopted a sensationalist style, complete with catchy headlines and images that livened up the typically dry newspaper style of the day. Circulation increased from under 5,000 to over 55,000 within three years after Heart's takeover, ending the Examiner's lengthy streak of losses.

When the Morning Journal was on the verge of bankruptcy in 1895, Hearst made the trip to New York City and bought it. Working-class, primarily immigrant readers had made the World the city's most popular newspaper, so he started vying with Pulitzer for their attention and financial support. Both newspapers ratcheted their sensationalist tactics to attract more readers and win the fierce competition.

At the turn of the century, the two publications' sensationalist reporting of Cuba's fight for independence from Spain prompted greater pressure on the United States government to interfere, leading to the outbreak of the Spanish-American War. Hearst, a prominent figure of the Progressive Era, campaigned for an eight-hour workweek and other changes aimed at improving workers' circumstances and reducing government corruption. Hearst's image as a defender of the common man against the ruling class helped propel the Journal's readership.

After being elected as a New York representative to Congress in 1902, Hearst made it his goal to become the party's nominee for president the following year. George, William Randolph, Jr., John, Randolph, and David were the five boys he and his ex-chorus girl wife Millicent Willson had the following year. Through purchasing newspapers in Chicago, Los Angeles, and Boston, he also sought to broaden the reach of his publishing company.

Hearst ran for the 1904 Democratic presidential nomination but was defeated by Alton B. Parker, who Theodore Roosevelt soundly defeated. Hearst was undeterred by this setback, and he eventually campaigned for mayor of New York City, where the formidable Tammany Hall political system soundly defeated him. Hearst never again served in an elected position after his lost bids for governor in 1906 and mayor in 1908.

He diverted his attention to his media empire, which grew to encompass newspapers in almost every major American city, as well as publications like Cosmopolitan, Good Housekeeping, Town & Country, Harper's Bazaar, and a wire service. The weekly newsreels and serialized dramatic films that Hearst produced were screened in movie theaters around the country. He was a fervent isolationist who used his media influence to push in vain for the neutrality of the US during WWI.

By 1925, Hearst had founded or bought newspapers throughout the United States and several periodicals. He had a longtime mistress named Marion Davies, who starred in films he produced and appeared in novels he wrote. In the 1920s, he constructed a magnificent castle on a 240,000-acre (97,000-hectare) estate in San Simeon, California, and he filled it with priceless artifacts from his extensive European travels.

In 1935, when his wealth was at its height, Hearst controlled dozens of media outlets, including a whopping 28 newspapers and 18 magazines, radio stations, film studios, and news agencies. As a result of his massive personal extravagances and the Great Depression of the 1930s forced him to sell failing newspapers or merge them with stronger companies. By 1940, the massive communications empire he had constructed was out of his control, and he had begun selling off pieces of his art collection as early as 1937. During his latter years, he essentially isolated himself from society. The film Citizen Kane was inspired by Hearst's life story (1941).

Chapter Four: The World vs. the Journal

The New York World

Cover of the New York World on Christmas of 1899 features a story by Mark Twain.

The term "yellow journalism" is used to denigrate news coverage that engages in unethical or unprofessional tactics such as scandal-mongering, sensationalism, jingoism, or other such behaviors. The word may allude to the years between 1895 and 1898 when Joseph Pulitzer's New

York World and William Randolph Hearst's New York Journal fought for readers' attention. Critics of both journals said they sensationalized the story in an effort to boost readership, despite the fact that both also provided legitimate reporting. In early 1897, the New York Press dubbed the newspapers of Pulitzer and Hearst "Yellow Journalism."

In spite of their heated rivalry, the World and the Journal were essentially the same in tone and style. They both invested massive resources into their Sunday publications, which acted like weekly magazines and went beyond the normal scope of daily journalism; both were Democrats; both were sympathetic to labor and immigrants (in contrast to publishers like the New York Tribune's Whitelaw Reid, who blamed their poverty on moral defects).

Many believe that sensationalist reporting and lies from Pulitzer and Hearst helped push the United States into the Spanish-American War. Although most Americans did not reside in New York City, those who held power there likely read more conservative publications like The New York Times, The New York Sun, and The Washington Post. Most notably, a legend is that painter Frederic Remington telegrammed Hearst to assure him that everything was calm in Cuba and that "There would be no war." In retaliation, Hearst "It is requested that you stay. You provide the imagery, and I'll provide the conflict." There is no other source for the tale outside the memoirs of reporter James Creelman, published in 1901, from which Orson Welles drew inspiration for making his picture Citizen Kane based on Hearst.

Nonetheless, Hearst became a war hawk when a revolt broke out in Cuba in 1895. It didn't take long for his front page to be dominated by stories of Cuban morality and Spanish violence. Even if his claims were shaky, 19th-century newspaper readers didn't need or prefer his articles to be 100% factual reporting. According to historian Michael Robertson, newspaper writers and readers of the 1890s "were far less concerned with discriminating between fact-based reporting, opinion, and literary."

Hearst's approach was more efficient since it singled out the bomb's perpetrator and promised a massive prize to its readers. Although Pulitzer did not have the same financial backing as Hearst, he maintained the story on the top page. However dire the situation on the island may have been, it was reported widely and incorrectly by the yellow press. Cuban peasants were forced into concentration camps by Spanish commander Valeriano Weyler, who was dispatched to the island to put down the uprising, further contributing to the economic crisis that had gripped the country. Hearst, demanding a confrontation for two years, claimed responsibility for starting it. He asked readers, "How do you enjoy the Journal's war?" one week after America went to war with Spain.

The idea that Hearst and Yellow Journalism were to blame for the war has been disproven by modern historians. While Republican publications like the Tribune and the New York Evening Post advocated moderation, President William McKinley never read the Journal. Newspapers outside of New York City did not follow the New York trend of "yellow journalism," according to industry scholars. Not only did the reports from the Journal and the World fail to get any attention outside of New York

City, but they were also not cited as sources by any of the top 10 regional newspapers. The public's revulsion at the violence and the realization by conservative leaders like McKinley that Spain had lost control of Cuba led to the outbreak of war. More so than the melodramatic stories in the New York Journal, these considerations occupied the president's attention.

At the 1900 presidential election, Hearst put his publications to work for the Democrats. He ran for president of his party later, but his reputation hit when writer Ambrose Bierce and editor Arthur Brisbane wrote letters calling for McKinley's murder. The Republican press flew into a frenzy when McKinley was shot on September 6, 1901, blaming Hearst for inspiring Leon Czolgosz to carry out the assassination. Even though Hearst claimed to have yanked Brisbane's column after its first publication and claimed not to be aware of Bierce's piece, the episode would plague him for the rest of his life and almost end any hopes he had of becoming president.

At the beginning of the century, Pulitzer took the World back to its crusading ways. Even after his passing in 1911, the World continued to be a progressive organ and the party's flagship journal until its extinction in 1931.

Chapter Five: Brooklyn Newsboys Strike of 1886

New York Evening Journal

The front page of the New York Evening Journal in 1911.

In New York, newsboys staged a series of strikes dating back to the 1890s, with the 1899 action being the most notable of these actions. Newsboys fought back on many occasions in the late 19th century, despite their youth and inexperience. Although tabloids often promoted the caricature of the street-smart, scrappy whelp, the industry's youngest personnel sometimes showed impressive levels of bloodthirsty pluck.

Due to the city's rapid expansion after the 1850s, newspaper publishers engaged in dishonorable and unjust commercial methods directed at the people who bought their journals. Selling newspapers was a tough profession with little pay. Because adults in New York City were seeking better-paying jobs elsewhere, newspapers typically turned to younger New Yorkers, mostly boys, to fill their ranks. Cynical publishers saw kids as a malleable labor force, which they took advantage of.

At first, the job's seeming need for autonomy seemed to hinder any type of organization, and newspapers apparently believed they could deliberately underpay their 'freelance' vendors, frequently putting gangs of newsboys against one other. In March 1886, a newspaper in Brooklyn across the East River carried such an error. This was before the city was consolidated.

In the middle of the 1800s, the rapidly growing city of Brooklyn necessitated the use of newsboys to distribute copies of the Brooklyn Times to new areas of the city. As the city expanded, it swallowed up several Long Island communities around the harbor, including what we now consider Brooklyn Heights and the Fulton Ferry. It grew in 1854 to include formerly unincorporated areas of Williamsburg and Bushwick. The Eastern District became a common name for these newly annexed areas. However, Brooklyn still had a lot of room to grow, and it gradually absorbed a number of communities to the south and southeast of its original limits, a region once known as the Western District and now including neighborhoods like Bay Ridge, Red Hook, and many more.

The Times offered a special bargain to newsboys in the Western District of Brooklyn to increase circulation in the city's developing neighborhoods. They would be given bundles of newspapers to read at a price one cent less per paper than what newsboys in the Eastern District were charging (one-and-a-fifth cent per paper). Having the Western District newsboys "push sales strongly in new areas" was seen by the Times' proprietors as a way to increase circulation. The newsboys in the Eastern District were furious when they learned this the next day.

The Brooklyn Daily Eagle reported on March 29 that a hundred newsboys armed with clubs and stones assaulted the Times distribution headquarters at South Eighth Street and attempted to stop two wagons of newspapers from traveling to the Western District. The youngsters were stopped by a wagon driver brandishing a whip and by incoming police officers, but one of the trucks was subsequently wrecked in what is now the Brooklyn Navy Yard neighborhood.

Several Williamsburg newsies flat-out refused when ordered to sell the Times by their elder, more cooperative peers. On their trip south, document-laden wagons were repeatedly ambushed. Many times, roaming gangs of youngsters "supported by a number of roughs" would attack a normal newsboy who was found peddling the Times. According to The Daily Eagle, some teenage newsboys are putting newspapers under their jackets to sell them to consumers without being seen.

The newsboy strike in Brooklyn lasted for a few days. The key to victory came from adult newspaper salespeople at traditional newsstands, much as it did in the later newsboys strike in 1899. The Times' wholesale price for newsboys in both parts of Brooklyn dropped to one cent per paper when a handful joined the boycott. On April 1, 1886, newsboys again took to the streets with ink-stained hands from selling copies of The New York Times and an optimistic outlook that their efforts would be rewarded with some additional cash.

Chapter Six: The Newsboys

The Newsboys
Newsies starts out with Sunday papers at 6 A.M.

The tenements and back alleys of American cities were overrun by swarms of homeless youth. Up to 12 percent of New York City's school-aged children were homeless in the 1870s, when they were believed to be between 20,000 and 30,000. A stack of newspapers was the only thing preventing thousands of people from going hungry. No one in authority cared about the newsboys' (and girls') meager earnings, so they were mostly left to fend for themselves. The "Newsies" would stock up on newspapers at deep discounts to resell to passersby. Still, others found gainful employment in bars and brothels. They had to stay up all night to ensure they sold every paper since they couldn't bring back the unsold ones. Despite their efforts, newsies only made roughly 30 cents an hour. Enough for a meal, to buy enough newspapers for the next day, and maybe even a 5-cent bed at the newsboy's house.

By the middle of the 19th century, newsboys were a common sight in major cities everywhere, selling newspapers to eager readers. Many young males in New York City either don't have families or are forced to find jobs because their own families can't afford to support them. Many American and other youngsters as young as seven or eight labor to help support their families. In the morning, the newsboys would get up bright and early to purchase the day's newspapers from the printer. Then, in an effort to eke out a living, they would lug their newspapers about the city and try to sell them at any cost. Things were tough, but they managed. Being a newsboy may be risky since rivalry often arises between the young men for control of the most prominent locations across the city. Using horses and carriages on the roadways only added to the risk.

Newsboys had no trouble selling papers to curious citizens during the Spanish-American War. There were other newspaper publishers in the city, but Joseph Pulitzer's The World and William Randolph Hearst's The Journal were the most prominent. Pulitzer and Hearst believed that people would pay more for newspapers during the war since they were vital to the public's survival. To attract the best writers and cartoonists, Pulitzer and Hearst competed with one another. Due to the lack of alternatives like television and the Internet, newspapers enjoyed widespread readership. The newspapers often fabricated news in an effort to boost sales. This kind of reporting, known as "Yellow Journalism," was dishonest.

After the conclusion of the Spanish-American War, fewer people bought newspapers, making life difficult for the newsboys. No matter how hard they tried, nobody seemed interested in purchasing their newspaper. The proprietors of newspapers have also raised prices, making them less affordable for readers. The newsboys realized they needed a strategy to win over newspaper owners and save their jobs. It would require a lot of hard work and perseverance to go up against newspaper proprietors like Joseph Pulitzer and William Randolph Hearst, who were highly strong guys with a lot of money.

Chapter Seven: The Strike

It's hard to pin down the exact moment or cause of the strike. The newsboys in Long Island City were the first to take action after learning that the Journal deliveryman had taken advantage of them. On July 18, in retaliation, they tipped over his wagon, stole his papers, and chased him out of town. feeling confident after their victory, the guys decided to take on the World and the Journal for fifty cents each hundred. In the past, this was the price. They informed their supply men that they would no longer purchase Hearst or Pulitzer papers and wanted a piece in return. News of the action in Long Island City spread swiftly to Manhattan, where a young man called Morris Cohen, who distributes approximately three hundred Worlds a day in City Hall Park, reportedly got a hold of the lads and persuaded them to strike. Don Seitz recounted all this in a letter to Pulitzer in Bar Harbor.

Regardless of what Seitz says, it's doubtful that Cohen was alone responsible for starting the strike in Manhattan. Each day around 4 o'clock, young boys who worked as newspaper vendors in the City Hall and Wall Street areas could be seen at City Hall Park and along Park Row, also known as Newspaper Row. While the majority were part-time students, there were also those who had dropped out of school to labor for a year or two until they turned 18 and could apply for better-paying jobs. Full-time hustlers peddled morning and early afternoon newspapers. The schoolboys joined them about three o'clock, just in time for the afternoon rush.

The lads' after-school chats throughout the spring and summer of 1899 likely included denunciations of Pulitzer and Hearst and suggestions of counterattack strategies. The downtown newsies may be summoned by Cohen, put down their red hots and crap games when they heard about the events in Long Island City, and gather at City Hall Park. On the afternoon of July 19, the union members stated they would go on strike the next day unless Pulitzer and Hearst reduced their fees. Delegates were sent out to inform the newsies of Fifty-ninth Street, Harlem, Brooklyn, Long Island City, and Jersey of the election of officials, the selection of a committee on discipline, and the discussion of strategy.

Afternoons during the first few days of the strike saw groups of downtown lads congregating in front of newspaper offices on Park Row in an attempt to physically block delivery wagons carrying newspapers to upper Manhattan and the suburbs from departing. On July 22, The Sun claimed that a hundred youths had gathered in Park Row at the time when the first editions of the "yellows" are normally released and that as soon as the wagons began, there was a huge howl and a rain of missiles that made the drivers' tasks difficult. As the police arrived, the youngsters dispersed, ostensibly because they had received orders not to harm the officers. In addition to their clubs, most youngsters had signs criticizing the scab extras and urging the public to boycott them taped to their headwear.

The same thing happened at many distribution sites. In Brooklyn, the newsboys formed committees to greet the delivery wagons. Any driver who tried to disobey them was showered with a carefully selected assortment of stones from the rebellious kids' bulging pockets. As the wagons arrived at the ferry, the Jersey City youths were there to tear up the papers tossed from the windows. The Yonkers organization sent scouts to intercept arriving trains and steal newspapers.

Chapter Eight: The Publisher's Action

The Journal and the World initially downplayed the strike's significance. After all, their rivals were only kids, too young, inexperienced, and carefree to stand a chance against grownups. When advertisers started asking for discounts on their bills because of the strike, the publishers finally got the hint about how serious the situation really was. The newsboys had won a PR war for public sympathy and were on their way to ending street distribution.

Within a few days, the strike halted paper circulation throughout Manhattan, from Wall Street to Fifty-ninth Street and Harlem, and from the East to the Hudson and the Hudson to the New Jersey cities of Long Island City, Brooklyn, Jersey City, and Newark. Newsboys in New York cities like Mount Vernon, Staten Island, Yonkers, Troy, and Rochester, as well as New Jersey cities like Plainfield, Trenton, Elizabeth, Paterson, and Asbury Park, as well as Connecticut cities like New Haven, Fall River, Massachusetts, and Providence, Rhode Island, joined the strike.

Every single one of those young boys was very serious about their strike. The fact that no publisher would take them seriously just served to motivate them more. They greeted the delivery wagons at the distribution stations every day, showered them with stones and rotten fruit, collected as many bundles as they could, and then marched up and down the streets with banners, pamphlets, songs, and shouts, happy of their achievement but always on the alert for any scab papers that may have slipped through.

The media, realizing the strike was serious for the first time, contacted political allies and police commanders for favors. On July 24, Seitz informed Pulitzer, "I went to headquarters and made plans to have the police break up certain striking spots tomorrow." The Journal, publishing editorials criticizing the police for their behavior during previous strikes, swiftly flipped its stance. The controversial articles, including a full-page attack on the police for being allies of monopoly, were removed from the paper. The Journal's editorial board, having recently adopted a pro-department stance, sent its editor to meet with Mayor Van Wyck to discuss increasing police presence in the city.

To get their publications out to the public, the publishers had to pay an army of scabs, thugs, and other toughs, requiring police protection for this force. When they ran out of adults to recruit, they despatched agents to Bowery hotels with a $2 per day plus commission offered to any male who would sell them copies of World or Journal. The agents led the youths inside the flophouses, where they could explain their situation. Only those who had found a method to earn two dollars without violating the strike showed up at the newspaper offices the next day. They discarded their bundles of newspapers as they left the building and then returned to the publishers to demand payment.

The boys knew how crucial public backing was. They took up a collection and used the eleven dollars they raised to print hundreds of circulars, which they distributed freely on the streets, at railway stations, on ferries, and in the non-struck newspapers. They held parades and public rallies and, wherever they could, spoke with reporters from the non-struck dailies to make their point.

The huge assembly at New Irving Hall on Broome Street was the high point of the two weeks for the lads and the public who read about their strike. Approximately 5,000 young boys from all over the city expressed their support. Frank Woods, the voice of the Polo Grounds and a former newsie, welcomed the 2,000 people who managed to fit inside the hall. The strikers were honored by a handful of local officials, songs were performed, the strikers applauded, and the scabs booed.

Chapter Nine: The End of the Strike

Dave Simmons

Photographed above is Dave Simmons selling newspapers. Dubbed Simons by newspapers, he was the Newspaperboys' union's first president.

As the lads stuck together for the remainder of that week and the next. The lads kept the World and Journal off the streets despite reports of scandal, a rushed trial, and the ouster of two strike leaders. In summing up the strike's impact on Pulitzer, Seitz acknowledged the significant decline in readership. While returns increased from 16% to 35%, the press run was cut from nearly 365,000 to 125,000. "It's incredible how far these young guys have come; our strategy of expelling adult males was counterproductive, but it was the only option. We needed to be represented, and the paper's departure was shocking."

After the demonstration, the newsboys adopted a new, less violent strategy. The strike was successful because the public was on their side and refused to purchase the World and Journal even after they stopped hitting persons who sold the publications. For the 26th of July, 1899, newsboys had planned a parade in which as many as 6,000 boys would march, followed by a band and fireworks, but the event was canceled owing to problems securing a permit.

On July 26, 1899, newsboys began spreading allegations that Kid Blink and David Simmons, two leaders of the strike, had sold out to newspaper bosses for money and agreed to sell the boycotting publications. Both boys rejected the allegations; however, it has been pointed out that Kid Blink seemed to have received a bribe, as he was dressed more formally than normal. Kid Blink and David Simmons resigned from their leadership posts in reaction to these rumors, with Simmons switching to the role of union treasurer and Blink becoming a "walking delegate."

The newsboys lost trust in their central leadership after hearing allegations that Kid Blink and David Simmons had abandoned the strike and when they were denied a parade permit. There were a few more newsboys who took the helm during the strikes, but none of them were as influential as Kid Blink had been.

During the second week of the strike, the publishers finally gave up and offered the guys a reasonable solution. The cost would stay the same, but unsold copies of the World and Journal would be gladly returned for a full refund. The young boys accepted the deal and returned to the streets on August 2nd.

Unfortunately, the newsboys' union didn't last long enough to claim triumph for its members. Near the end, just the leaders and their press pronouncements remained. The union's efforts to initiate the strike, convene the massive gathering, and disseminate information to the lads and the public were heroic. However, as the boycott gained momentum, its end was inevitable. The citywide organization was mostly idle throughout the strike because of its lack of control over its operations. The newsboys patrolled their respective areas. All the factions saw themselves as part of the bigger picture, but they weren't willing to accept judgments made by those in other districts.

It's possible that the union might be strengthened or at least given some work if the publishers had engaged officially with the group. Nonetheless, the publishers chose to disregard the union, which, from their point of view, was probably the best course of action. When they decided to make peace with the lads, they simply informed the circulation and branch office managers that they would accept complete refunds. The guys agreed to the terms without holding a vote or making a formal decision and stood in line to purchase their papers.

Chapter Ten: Fair Labor Standards Act

Child labor

Tony and Charlie, a pair of six-year-old newsies.

The newsboys' strike was a turning point in the struggle for better working conditions in the United States. Twenty years later, young workers in coal mines and textile factories also went on strike. The strikes brought attention to the difficult working circumstances that many children suffer. The United States Fair Labor Standards Act was established in 1938 by the country's legislative body. Young people around the nation are now required to be a certain age before beginning employment, and their hours on the job are capped.

Workers in the United States are guaranteed a minimum wage and "time and a half" for any hours worked in excess of 40 per week under the Fair Labor Standards Act of 1938 (FLSA). It also outlaws the use of "oppressive child labor," which refers to the forced work of children. Unless an employer can demonstrate an exception from coverage, it applies to workers involved in interstate commerce or employed by a business that engages in trade or manufacturing commodities for commerce.

Senator Hugo Black developed the Fair Labor Standards Act in 1932, and his plan to mandate companies to adopt a thirty-hour workweek was greeted with strong opposition. A revised version of Black's idea was finally approved in 1938. Several influential figures, such as Frances Perkins, Clara Mortenson Beyer of the Bureau of Labor Standards at the United States Department of Labor, and Congresswoman Mary T. Norton, were crucial in bringing about the new version.

The Fair Labor Standards Act was formally enacted on June 25, 1938, by President Franklin D. Roosevelt. The law had a rocky ride in the House and the Senate, and Roosevelt signed it along with 120 others on a Saturday, nine days after Congress had closed. However, the sectors it applied to employed only approximately one-fifth of the workforce.

In its final form, the act, which Secretary of Labor Frances Perkins largely drafted, prohibited all work for children under the age of 14 and hazardous work for children 14-18; established "a minimum hourly wage of 25 cents and a maximum workweek of 44 hours (to be adjusted to 40 hours by Oct. 23, 1940)"; and guaranteed "time and a half" for certain jobs. The Fair Labor Standards Act (FLSA) is perhaps the most convoluted employment legislation. Most amendments have enlarged the law's scope or modified the minimum wage to reflect inflation.

The Fair Labor Standards Act defines whether an employee is considered "on the clock" or not entitled to compensation. Determining whether an employee is exempt or nonexempt from the FLSA's overtime laws is complicated. All hours worked in excess of 40 in a seven-day workweek must be compensated for at one and a half times the usual hourly rate ("time-and-a-half"), as mandated by law.

Employees whose employers participate in interstate commerce or in manufacturing products for commerce are covered by the FLSA, as are workers employed by a business engaged in commerce or producing goods for commerce. Workers in the domestic service sector (such as housekeepers, cooks, and full-time babysitters) are also covered by the Fair Labor Standards Act (FLSA), along with those in the healthcare and education sectors (including at hospitals, schools for children with special needs or those with exceptional abilities, and educational institutions of all types, from daycare centers to universities). Since independent contractors and volunteers are not employees, the FLSA does not provide them rights.

Millions of youngsters had to labor to help their families got by a century ago. The use of children as workers dates back centuries. Beyond shifts in tasks and levels of automation, the way individuals feel about labor is the most noticeable difference. Time, location, social hierarchy, and economic standing all have a role. It is a more recent trend to disapprove of employing youngsters in physically demanding jobs for extended periods of time. A century and a half ago in the United States, children worked without the safety net that is now guaranteed by federal law.

Discussion Questions 1

⁓꧁꧂⁓

The Spanish–American War boosted newspaper sales; thus, numerous newspapers raised newsboy bundles from 50 to 60 cents. In what manner did the Spanish-American War increase newspaper sales? Why did the price of newsboy bundles increase?

Discussion Questions 2

Except for the World and Journal, most papers cut prices to 50 cents as sales plummeted. Why have newspaper sales decreased? Why did the World and Journal not reduce the price of their newspaper to fifty cents?

Discussion Questions 3

Long Island City newsboys overturned a delivery cart and protested against the World and Journal. How did the little lads cause the distribution wagon to overturn? How did they get other lads to join their cause?

Discussion Questions 4

After the Long Island City strike, Manhattan, Brooklyn, and other newsboys followed. How did the newsies execute their citywide strike in New York? What impact did this strike have on the New York populace?

Discussion Questions 5

Newsboys used violence to prevent paper sales for a few days following the strike. How aggressive were the youngsters during the strike's first days? In your opinion, how did these youngsters learn to commit such brutal crimes?

Discussion Questions 6

Males found selling the World or Journal were assaulted, and their papers were burned frequently without police assistance. Would you consider this newsies behavior to be justifiable? Why do you say so?

Discussion Questions 7

Nearly eight thousand New York newsboys attended an Irving Hall rally. What transpired during the rally? How did this gathering affect the ongoing newsboy strike?

Discussion Questions 8

The World and Journal rejected their terms but proposed a compromise: the newsboy bundle would continue at 60 cents, but any unsold papers would be purchased back. Do you believe this deal is fair? Why did the newsboys accept these conditions instead of negotiating their own?

True or False Questions

1. **True or False:** The 1899 newsboys' strike was led by U.S. youth to modify how Joseph Pulitzer and William Randolph Hearst's newspapers paid its newsboys. The strikes blocked the circulation of the two journals and news dissemination in several New England communities for many days in New York City. Although paper prices were not dropped, the strike forced the World and Journal to provide full buybacks to their sellers, boosting newsies' pay.

2. **True or False:** Newsboys distributed newspapers in the early 1900s. Afternoon editions were sold almost entirely by newsboys, while morning copies were given directly to subscribers. Most newsboys were impoverished immigrants who sold papers afternoons and nights after school.

3. **True or False:** The Spanish–American War increased newspaper sales in 1898; thus, numerous publishers boosted the price of a newsboy's bundle of 100 newspapers

from 50 to 60. Sales offset this price hike. The Evening World and New York Evening Journal were the only publications to raise prices after the war.

4. **True or False:** The newsboys were aggressive in the early days of the strike. Strikers would assault and demolish anybody peddling the two boycotting periodicals. The newspaper proprietors recruited adult men to sell their papers with police protection, but the strikes frequently distracted the policemen from getting at the "scabs."

5. **True or False:** Senator Timothy D. Sullivan staged a citywide newsboy demonstration at Irving Hall on July 24, 1899. Five thousand Manhattan lads, two thousand Brooklyn boys, and several hundred from other parts of the city attended the demonstration. Local lawmakers and business people addressed the audience.

6. **True or False:** After the rally, newsboys were mostly non-violent. Even when they stopped hitting World and Journal sellers, the strike was successful because the public supported them and refused to purchase the publications. Due to permission complications, the newsboys organized a procession on July 26, 1899, with 6,000 boys, a band, and fireworks.

7. **True or False:** On July 26, 1899, newsboys heard that strike organizers Kid Blink and David Simmons had sold the boycotting publications for a fee from newspaper bosses. Both youths rejected the claims, although Kid Blink wore finer clothing than normal, suggesting a bribe. In response to these concerns, Kid Blink and David Simmons resigned from their leadership roles.

8. **True or False:** On August 1, 1899, the World and Journal offered the newsboys a compromise: a hundred papers

would cost 60, but they would buy back any unsold papers. This meant that the boys, who had problems selling all their papers, would not have to sell late into the night to avoid a loss for the day. On August 2, 1899, the newsboys accepted this settlement, stopped the strike, and dissolved.

True or False Answer

1. **True**
2. **True**
3. **True**
4. **True**
5. **True**
6. **True**
7. **True**
8. **True**

Conclusion

The newsies were extraordinary because they were determined to make a difference by forming their own union and facing up against newspaper magnates. Typically, orphaned boys, the newsies made a livelihood selling newspapers on the street for a few cents a day. Those of higher socioeconomic status sometimes resorted to wearing thin clothes, light coats, and caps since it was all they could afford to wear while living paycheck to paycheck. Some of them braced the cold weather while clothed in filthy rags and without proper footwear or outerwear. Despite the weather, there was no stopping the little lads from making the daily trek to the publishing houses, rain or shine, to buy newspapers. The newsboys would take various routes in order to reach their consumers.

Poor working conditions were a constant reality for newsies. They spent the whole day on their feet, scurrying all over the metropolis. Young boys still in their developmental stages had a tough time with the extended hours, most of which occurred during daylight hours. These kids spent their days attempting to make a living as newspaper vendors at brothels, saloons, and other seedy establishments instead of being in class. Forgoing the chance to earn a living via one's education directly resulted from this. Seeing young individuals, mostly boys, delivering newspapers door-to-door in New York City raised awareness of child labor and brought attention to the city's high concentration of urban poor.

A growing number of employees organized into unions around the turn of the century in order to better represent their interests in negotiations. Nonetheless, trade unions were still formative, and adults formed and documented each. Although they did not formally form a labor union, the newsboys of New York City effectively organized a strike that included workers from all five boroughs. These youngsters disseminated information and banded together to negotiate with newspaper publishers as a union of newspaper boys. The newsies' strike was notable for its public demonstration of young solidarity and the issue of child labor.

The newsboys were an important organization that stood up to wealthy industrialists and financiers at the turn of the century. Despite their age, they were certain that if they struck together, they could have their voices heard. They had no fear of anybody, not even more experienced merchants. Instead of acting like typical, shy little lads, the newsies marched throughout the city with banners and picket placards. People did not anticipate that this impoverished and elderly bunch would rise up and go on strike.

Some may say that the newsboys' lives have not improved since before. There was no improvement in their working conditions or salary following the walkout. But notwithstanding the past, this strike opened the door to better conditions by highlighting the problem. In order to prevent the waste of money, newsboys were compensated daily for unsold newspapers. They might attempt to recoup their investment in unsold newspapers if they needed to raise funds for necessities like food and clothing.

The Newsies were a formidable organization that helped bring attention to the problem of child labor by demonstrating that young employees could successfully demonstrate their solidarity in front of the public. Poor and destitute, the newsboys scraped by. The newsies became targets of abuse and robberies because of the sympathy people had for them. The health and education of newsies were hampered by the long hours they worked and the unpredictable nature of the weather. By convincing municipal authorities that child labor is a problem, the newsies were able to gain reimbursement for newsies all throughout the city. The newsies stood together and shifted public opinion, leading to more support for legislation to end child labor.

Bibliography (Works Cited)

1. Fraga, K., The True Story Of The 1899 Newsboy Strike That Saw Newsies Take On Publishing Tycoons — And Win (October 6, 2021). All That's Interesting, <https://allt hatsinteresting.com/newsboy-strike-of-1899>

2. The Newsboys Strike of 1899, Background (n.d.). <https://newsboysstrike1899.weebly.com/background -story.html>

3. Santullo, K. M., Newspaper Strike of 1899 (November 7, 2017). History of the City of New York, <https://blogs.sh u.edu/nyc-history/2017/11/07/newspaper-strike-of-19 00/>

4. Dellinger, J., Joseph Pulitzer: Biography, Accomplish-ments, and Quotes (n.d.). Study.com, <https://study.co m/learn/lesson/joseph-pulitzer-accomplishments-quot es.html>

5. History, William Randolph Hearst (November 30, 2021). <https://www.history.com/topics/early-20th-century-u

s/william-randolph-hearst>

6. Britannica, William Randolph Hearst (n.d.). <https://www.britannica.com/biography/William-Randolph-Hearst>

7. Wikipedia, History of American newspapers (n.d.). <https://en.wikipedia.org/wiki/History_of_American_newspapers#Postwar_trends>

8. The Bowery Boys, Before 'Newsies': The Brooklyn Newsboys Strike of 1886 (March 28, 2012). <https://www.boweryboyshistory.com/2012/03/before-newsies-brooklyn-newsboys-strike.html#:~:text=On%20March%2029th%2C%20according%20to,heading%20to%20the%20Western%20District.>

9. Today in History, February 23, 1908 Newsies (February 23, 2019). <https://todayinhistory.blog/tag/newsboy-strike/>

10. Bedtime History Stories, History of the Newsboys or Newsies Strike of 1899 for Kids (n.d.). <https://bedtimehistorystories.com/newsboys-newsies-strike-of-1899-for-kids/>

11. Kenton, W., Fair Labor Standards Act (FLSA) Overview and History (September 1, 2022). Investopedia, <https://www.investopedia.com/terms/f/fair-labor-standards-act-flsa.asp>

12. Wikipedia, Fair Labor Standards Act of 1938 (n.d.). <https://en.wikipedia.org/wiki/Fair_Labor_Standards_Act_of_1938#Tipping>

Images (License-Free)

Joseph Pulitzer

A portrait of Joseph Pulitzer. To view a copy of this license, visit https://www.metmuseum.org/art/collection/search/421565.

William Randolph Hearst

A portrait of William Randolph Hearst. To view a copy of this license, visit http://history.sandiego.edu

The New York World

Cover of the New York World on Christmas of 1899 features a story by Mark Twain. To view a copy of this license, visit http://www.slate.com/id/2126420

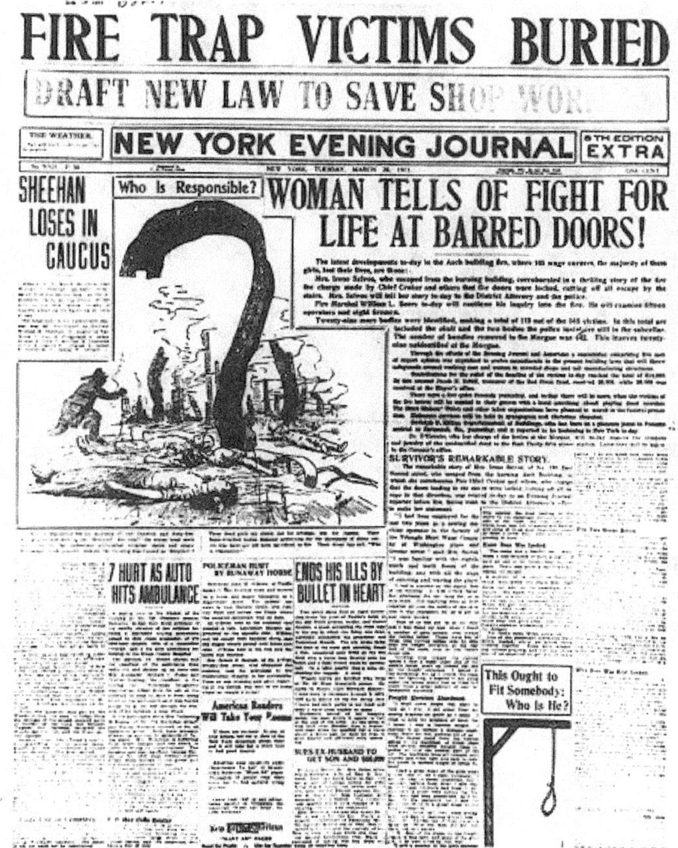

New York Evening Journal

The front page of the New York Evening Journal in 1911. To view a copy of this license, visit https://www.flickr.com/photos/kheelcenter/5279752692/

The Newsboys

Newsies starts out with Sunday papers at 6 A.M. To view a copy of this license, visit http://hdl.loc.gov/loc.pnp/nclc.0331 3

Child labor

Tony and Charlie, a pair of six-year-old newsies. To view a copy of this license, visit http://hdl.loc.gov/loc.pnp/nclc.0391 8

"DAVE" SIMONS,
The deposed president of the Newsboys' Union.

Dave Simmons

Photographed above is Dave Simmons selling newspapers. Dubbed Simons by newspapers, he was the Newspaperboys' union's first president. To view a copy of this license, visit https://www.loc.gov/resource/sn83030214/1899-07-30/ed-1/?sp=26&st=image&r=-0.155,0.169,0.801,0.3,0